熱帶雨林

Sharing the Planet | Non-Fiction Series

Copyright © 2022 by Level Learning, INC. and Washington Yu Ying PCS™
Original and Edited Text Copyright © 2022 by Washington Yu Ying PCS™

All rights reserved. No part of this book in whole or part may be reproduced without written permission from the publisher.

Published by Level Learning, INC.
Content Contributors:
Washington Yu Ying PCS™ - Qianyi (Shirley) Zhang, Pearl Zao He You
Level Learning - Jingyao Qi

Illustrations by: Josh Taira

Leveling classification based on Level Learning standard. For full description, visit www.levellearning.com

ISBN 978-1-64040-073-3
Traditional Chinese Edition

About Level Learning:
Level Learning provides a literacy focused curriculum specifically designed for K-12 Chinese as a Second Language classrooms. Our program offers 20 levels of specific and detailed objectives, leveled texts and passages, mastery-based online assessment, and analytics to enable data-driven instruction. Level Learning reading curriculum for both literature and informational text emphasize grammar and comprehension skills to help teachers develop confident and independent Chinese language readers. The non-fiction series of books are specifically designed to support our informational text course based on multiple national standards. To learn more about our entire offering, visit www.levellearning.com.

About Washington Yu Ying PCS™:
Washington Yu Ying PCS is a Mandarin English dual language immersion International Baccalaureate (IB) World school. Yu Ying's mission is to inspire and prepare young people to create a better world by challenging them to reach their full potential in a nurturing Chinese/English educational environment. Yu Ying's comprehensive IB, dual immersion curriculum equips students with global competencies for success in the real world. As a leader in immersion education, Yu Ying is determined to advance Chinese language programs and global citizenry education by helping other schools create and strengthen their Chinese programs. For more information, email: products@washingtonyuying.org

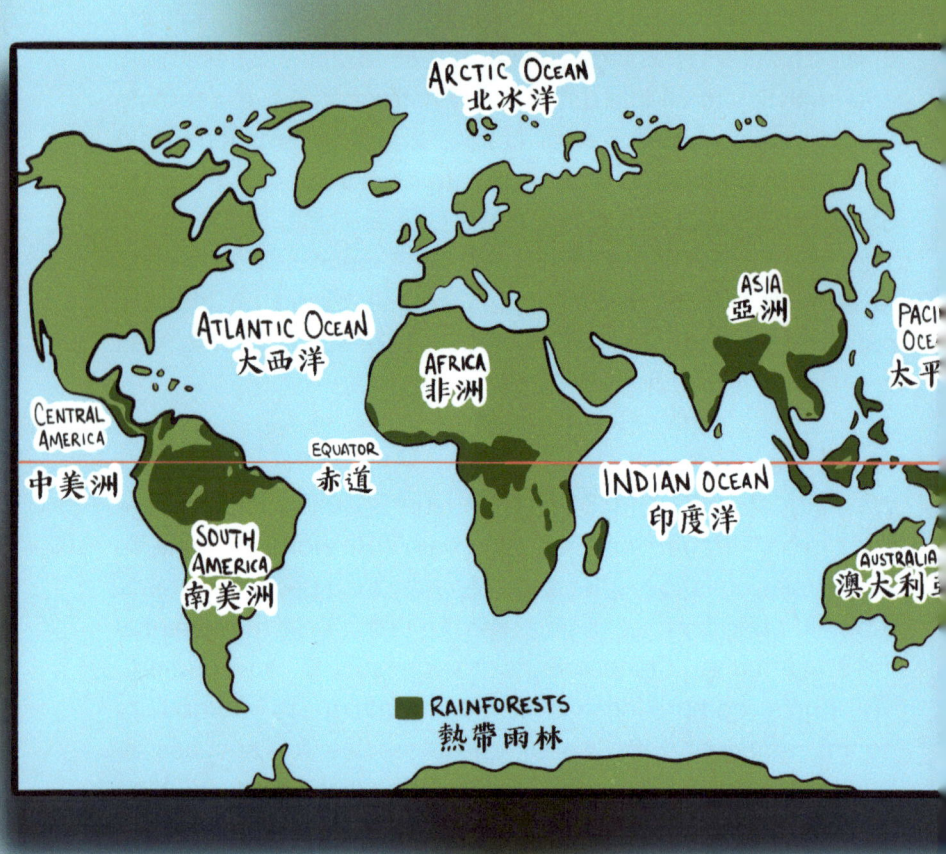

什麼是熱帶雨林呢？熱帶雨林氣候炎熱，雨水充足，沒有明顯的季節變化。在非洲、亞洲、澳洲、中美洲和南美洲都有熱帶雨林。

雖然熱帶雨林只佔全球面積的百分之二，但是在這裡生長著全世界一半以上的植物和動物。在這裡，你可以看到十幾層樓高的大樹，巨大的芭蕉樹葉，以及各種各樣罕見的植物。

世界上最大的熱帶雨林是南美洲的亞馬遜雨林。它橫跨9個國家，面積700萬平方公里。這裡是成千上萬野生動植物的家。除了豐富的植物，亞馬遜雨林裡也生活著很多罕見的動物，比如說粉色的海豚，藍色的有劇毒的樹蛙等等。

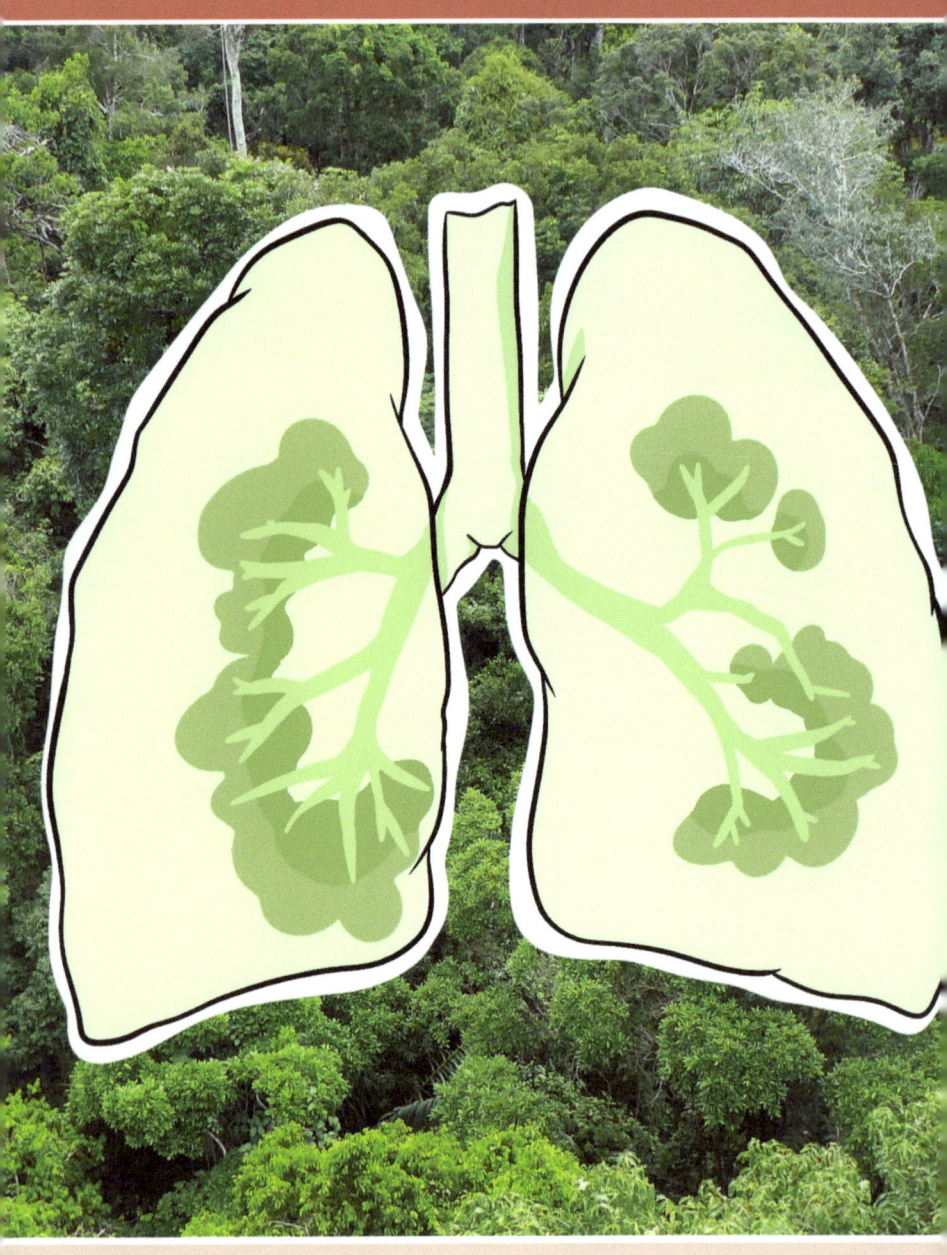

你知道亞馬遜雨林被稱為「地球之肺」嗎？這是因為大面積的雨林吸收了地球上大量的二氧化碳，又釋放出了很多氧氣。就像人和動物呼吸一樣，地球的呼吸要靠這些熱帶雨林。

然而，近幾十年，熱帶雨林的面積正在快速減少。造成面積減少的主要原因是人們砍伐了大量雨林中的樹木。其次，還有大面積的雨林被變成了養牛場或農田。科學家指出，如果亞馬遜雨林消失，地球將會減少釋放三分之一的氧氣。

保護熱帶雨林，我們可以做些什麼呢？我們可以節約用紙，比如可以多使用回收紙，這樣就不需要砍伐那麼多的樹木來造紙；我們也應該減少食物浪費，特別是肉和奶製品，這樣就不用把雨林變成養牛場了。

不僅如此，我們還要告訴身邊的家人和朋友，讓更多人知道保護雨林的重要性。讓我們大家行動起來，一起保護珍貴的熱帶雨林！

Glossary

	Pinyin	English Definition
熱帶	rè dài	tropical
雨林	yǔ lín	rainforest
氣候	qì hòu	climate, weather
炎熱	yán rè	hot
充足	chōng zú	plenty
明顯	míng xiǎn	obvious
季節	jì jiē	seasons
變化	biàn huà	change
非洲	fēi zhōu	Africa
亞洲	yà zhōu	Asia
澳洲	ào zhōu	Australia
中美洲	zhōng měi zhōu	Central America
南美洲	nán měi zhōu	South America
佔	zhàn	to occupy
面積	miàn jī	area

	Pinyin	English Definition
百分之二	bǎi fèn zhī èr	2 percent
層	céng	floor, story
芭蕉	bā jiāo	banana
罕見	hǎn jiàn	rare
亞馬遜	yà mǎ xùn	Amazon
橫跨	héng kuà	stretch over
平方公里	píng fāng gōng lǐ	square kilometer
成千上萬	chéng qiān shàng wàn	thousands and thousands
野生	yě shēng	wild
豐富	fēng fù	rich, plentiful
海豚	hǎi tún	dolphin
劇毒	jù dú	toxic
樹蛙	shù wā	tree frog
肺	fèi	lung
吸收	xī shōu	to absorb

Glossary

	Pinyin	English Definition
二氧化碳	èr yǎng huà tàn	carbon dioxide
釋放	shì fàng	to release
氧氣	yǎng qì	oxygen
呼吸	hū xī	to breathe
然而	rán ér	however
快速	kuài sù	high speed
減少	jiǎn shǎo	to reduce
砍	kǎn	to chop
養牛場	yǎng niú chǎng	cattle farm
科學家	kē xué jiā	scientist
保護	bǎo hù	to protect
節約	jié yuē	to save
回收	huí shōu	recyclable
造	zào	to make
紙	zhǐ	paper

	Pinyin	English Definition
浪費	làng fèi	to waste
奶	nǎi	milk
製品	zhì pǐn	product
不僅如此	bù jǐn rú cǐ	not only
行動	xíng dòng	to take action